Options trading strategies

A beginner's guide on all to know strategies, easy and complete instruction to options trading to turn 2k into 20k with technical analysis and risk management.

Written By

Matthew Morris

Table of Contents

INTRODUCTION

Thank you for purchasing this book!

Options are an attractive investment tool. They have a risk/reward framework, which is unlike any other. They can be used in a multitude of combinations that make them very versatile. The risk factor involved can be diluted by using these options with other financial instruments or other option contracts, and at the same time, opening more avenues for profits. While many investments have an unbound quantum of risk attached, options' trading, on the other hand, has defined risks, which the buyers know about.

Enjoy your reading!

Chapter 1: Risks That You Need to Avoid

Understanding Options Risks

O ptions trading process does carry some risks with it. Understanding these risks and taking mitigating steps will make you not just a better trader but a more profitable one as well. A lot of traders love options trading because of the immense leverage that this kind of trading affords them. Should an investment work out as desired, then the profits are often quite high. With stocks, you can expect returns of between 10%, 15%, or even 20%. However, when it comes to options, profit margins over 1,000% are very possible.

Basically, these kinds of trades are very possible due to the nature and leverage offered by options. A savvy trader realizes that he or she can control an almost equivalent number of shares as a traditional stock investor, but at a fraction of the cost. Therefore, when you invest in options, you can spend a tiny amount of money to control a large number of shares. This kind of leverage limits your risks and exposure compared to a stock investor.

As an investor or trader, you should never spend more than 3% to 5% of your funds in any single trade. For instance, if you have $10,000 to invest, you should not spend more than $300 to $500 on any trade.

Also, as a trader, you are not just mitigating against potential risks, but are also looking to take advantage of the leverage. This is also known as gaining a professional trader's edge. While it is crucial to reduce the risk through careful analysis and selection of trades, you should also aim to make huge profits and enjoy big returns on your trades. There will always be some losses, and as a trader, you should get to appreciate this. However, your major goal as a trader should be to ensure that your wins are much, much larger than any losses that you may suffer.

All types of investment opportunities carry a certain level of risk. However, options trading carries a much higher risk of loss. Therefore, ensure that you have a thorough understanding of the risks and always be on the lookout.

Risk #1: Time Is Not on Your Side

You need to keep in mind that all options have an expiration date and that they do expire in time. When you invest in stocks, time is on your side most of the time. However, things are different when it comes to options. Basically, the closer that an option gets to its expiration, the quicker it loses its value and earning potential.

Options deterioration is usually rather rapid, and it accelerates in the last days until expiration. Basically, as an investor, ensure that you only invest dollar amounts that you can afford to lose. The good news though, is that there are a couple of actions that you can take in order to get things on your side.

- Trade mostly in options with expiration dates that are within the investment opportunity.

- Buy options at or very near the money.

- Sell options any time you think volatility is highly-priced.

- Buy options when you are of the opinion that volatility is underpriced.

Risk #2: Prices Can Move Pretty Fast

Options are highly leveraged financial instruments. Because of this, prices tend to move pretty fast. Basically, options prices can move huge amounts within minutes and sometimes even seconds. This is unlike other stock market instruments, like stocks, that move-in hours and days.

Small movements in the price of a stock can have huge implications on the value of the underlying stock. You need to be vigilant and monitor price movements often. However, you can generate profits without monitoring activity on the markets twenty-four hours a day.

As an investor or trader, you should seek out opportunities where chances of earning a significant profit are immense. The opportunity should be sufficiently robust so that pricing by seconds will be of little concern. In short, search for opportunities that will lead to large profits even when you are not accurate when selling.

When structuring your options, you should ensure that you use the correct strike prices as well as expiration months in order to cut out most of the risk. You should also consider closing out your trades well before the expiration of options. This way, time value will not dramatically deteriorate.

Risk #3: Naked Short Positions Can Result in Substantial Losses

Anytime that your naked short option presents a high likelihood of substantial and sometimes even unlimited losses, shorting put naked means selling stock options with no hedging of your position.

When selling a naked short, it simply implies that you are actually selling a call option, or even a put option, but without securing it using an option position, a stock or cash. It is advisable to sell a put or a call in combination with other options or with stocks. Remember that whenever you short sell a stock, you are, in essence, selling borrowed stock. Sooner or later, you will have to return the stock.

Fortunately, with options, there is no borrowing of stock or any other security.

Chapter 2: The Option Trader Mindset

When it comes to trading successfully every single day, if you let your emotions dictate your actions, you will never find the success you seek. Instead, you will need to develop the type of emotionless mindset that makes the best options traders so successful. Following the suggestions outlined below will allow you to focus on long term success regardless of what distractions are currently taking place around you. Studies show that as little as 10 percent of options traders have the right mindset to cultivate success in the long term, changing your mindset is the first step to ensuring you are one of them.

Manage Expectations

The first thing that is required if you hope to develop the mindset of a successful options trader is to understand just what to expect when it comes to the results of your early day trading experiences. Only by tempering your expectations of major successes in a short period will you be able to prevent the types of negative emotions that can lead to negative trades in the long term. It is important to understand what types of emotions you are going to feel regularly, so that you can more adequately control your responses.

When you first start out, it may be helpful to keep a journal of your individual trades as well as the resulting emotions you felt, both on the good trades and the bad. It is important to know what you expect as you go through your standard trading process, so that you can be prepared to rationally counter any emotions that you might expect to encounter. Only by completely keeping your emotions in check will you be able to put the plan you will ultimately create into action and not vary from it no matter what.

The biggest cause for emotional concern comes from the fact that many new options traders view trading as if it should always produce the desired results when a plan is followed correctly. This is, in fact, not the case and even when you do come up with a winning plan, it will not be 100 percent successful. Understanding that losses are a very real part of the daily trading game is the first step to keeping your emotions regarding every loss in check. To mitigate these feelings, it is important to understand that a good trade is not one that made money but rather one that followed your system to the letter.

Find a System

Once you find a system that works for you, either by creating one uniquely from scratch or finding the published work of a master trader and putting it to work for you, it will be important to stick with it until you reach the recommended number of trades before tweaking a single variable and then repeating the process.

While it may be difficult to jump ship immediately if the results of a specific system don't work out, in reality, it is much more beneficial in the long term to instead determine just why the system in question worked for someone else but did not work for you. A major evidence in your evolution as an options trader will be the moments you can see why the trader who struck it rich after a few random trades is actually less successful than a trader with a few different plans that are always executed properly no matter what. In the long term, a reliable strategy is one that is infinitely more profitable than any single trade, no matter how lucrative.

Viewing options trading as a marathon, not a sprint, is crucial to your long-term growth as a trader and has the added benefit of making every losing trade a valuable learning experience instead of one that is an abject failure. This will help you keep your spirits up, and your resolution to your system in check, throughout all the natural ups and downs the market is likely going to bestow upon you. Keeping this unilaterally positive mindset will also give you an edge over the competition who will, statistically speaking, probably let their emotions alter their system in real-time, which will ultimately cost them greatly, if not in the short term, then definitely in the long term.

Understand When Not to Exercise or Trade Out

If you plan on trading successfully in the long term, then you need to develop a mindset that encourages inaction as a probable road to success. Just because you have gone ahead and created either a call or a pull, doesn't mean you have to do anything with it, as long as you are not the writer. While this should seem explicit to anyone in the calm light of a hypothetical situation, it is actually something that many new traders commonly forget once the stress of actually having money in the mix is added into the equation.

Every single successful trader has determined exactly when they should go through with a trade and when they should not exercise an option. The answer should be clear by now, successful traders listen to their systems and don't let the fact that they have an actual profit (or loss) on the line deter them from making the correct choice every single time. It can be difficult to keep a cool head, especially amid numerous losses in a short time; conversely, this is also the time you need to keep a true option trader mindset as doing otherwise is akin to giving in to the temptation to go off plan and pay for it even more heavily.

You Cannot Overvalue Patience

You cannot be a successful options trader unless you have the patience to wait for the right moment to execute every trade. This means personally reinforcing the notion that the market doesn't move immediately and even the most volatile options will require time to build up steam. Likewise, it is important to never let your focus be exclusively on a single trade as doing so will only artificially inflate the importance of that trade in your mind, which will make it easier for emotions to take over at a critical moment.

Those who are serious about becoming regular options traders need to focus on the fact that every individual trade is only a small part of the overall goal of being a successful trader and treat it with the relevant amount of care. A major part of being a patient trader is, likewise, knowing that some days are simply not worth the risk or effort of trading and that overtrading is just as hazardous as not taking advantage of positive trade conditions when they do materialize.

This is why it is important to only set weekly or monthly expectations and to never try and reach a goal amount at the end of every trading day. Even if you do end up making the target amount of trades each day to hit your goal, likely, at least some of these trades will not have stood up to the strict level of scrutiny that a good plan requires. Stick with making only the right types of trades and your weekly or monthly average will take care of itself, if not, then you can think about changing your plan.

Be Ready to Adapt

The successful options traders know when to follow their plans, but they also know that no plan will be the right choice, even if early indicators say otherwise. There is a difference between making a point of sticking to a plan, following it blindly; and knowing when to take other alternatives; it can mean success or abject failure. It is important to be aware of when and where experimentation and new ideas are appropriate and when it is best to toe the line and gather more data in order to make a well-reasoned decision.

Likewise, an adaptive options trader knows that market conditions can change unexpectedly and is prepared to respond accordingly. This means understanding when the time is right to go in a new direction, regardless of the potential risks that doing so might entail. Sometimes a good trader has to make a leap of faith, and a trader who is successful in the long term knows what signs to look for that indicate this type of scenario is occurring in real-time. Unfortunately, this type of foresight cannot be taught, and instead must be found with experience.

Prioritize Consistency

If you ever hope to develop the type of mindset that allows professional options traders to be successful, you will need to understand how important it is to be consistent in your trades, not just in theory, but in practice. To reach this point, however, you will likely need to deal with both subpar gains as well as financial setbacks. To alter the rate at which either of these occurs, you need to not just experience gains but understand why those trades proceeded in the way that they did. Being inquisitive when it comes to your gains is just as important as analyzing your errors when it comes to your long-term success.

While more volatile traders are interested in scenarios that offer great rewards and ever greater risks, options traders that tend to be successful across the long term understand that the most reliable way is to focus on trades with medium or small returns that turn around reliably time and time again. An occasional outstanding return is nice, but it is no way to build a steady trade record. What's more, a system that works on mediocre trades is also more likely to work on more substantial variations as well, test your system thoroughly before putting it to work on a major trade.

Know Yourself

A good options trader understands their own strengths and weaknesses when it comes to trading and looks for systems that maximize their strengths and minimizes their weaknesses. There is no one perfect system that is right for everybody in any given situation, no matter how much easier it would make things if there were. This is another reason it is so important to keep a journal during your early days of trading so you can look for certain repeating tendencies that you may want to factor into your system choosing process.

Likewise, this will help you to understand when you are becoming emotional or approaching a trade in the wrong way. While at first, it will be helpful to have an outline of what types of emotions to expect in given situations, with enough practice you will find you can tell when you are becoming emotional, even without the cheat sheet. If you find yourself having difficulty with this part of the mindset building exercise, you may find it helpful to simply take a break and come back later. Focusing too thoroughly on a problem can lead to just as many problems as it may potentially solve. Focus on keeping a clear mind and you will find that not only is it easier to focus on sticking to your system, but that you are more easily able to determine the specific causes for the success or failure found in every trade. Practice keeping this mindset during every trade and you will see a greater percentage of successful trades sooner than you may expect.

Chapter 3: The Best Strategies to Invest with Call and Put Options Trading

Selling Call Options

N ow we are going to shift gears and consider selling options for income rather than buying options hoping to profit by trading. Many traders prefer selling options. Although there are risks, selling options is actually a more reliable approach for earning money than trying to speculate with trading. There is still a level of speculating when you are selling options, but the speculation is one-sided, making it less risky. We will see how this works in a minute.

Covered Call

The simplest way to sell options for income is by using covered calls. To sell a covered call, you must own 100 shares of stock for each option that you want to sell. So, if you have been investing in some of your favorite stocks over the years and you have built up some shares, you can start earning money off the shares by selling call options against them.

The strategy involves selling the options with a strike price that is out of the money. If you sell in the money options, while you are going to be able to get a nice payment, your options will be "called away" if they expire in the money, and there is even a risk a buyer might exercise the option before expiration. So, beginning traders are better off selling out of the money options, even though you earn less money.

The money you are paid for selling an option is called the premium. This is analogous to an insurance premium, and many people trading stocks invest in options for insurance. This is especially true to get protection against falling stock prices, buying a put option can give you insurance by giving you the out of being able to sell the stock at the strike price of the put if prices drop significantly.

With a covered call, you find the option that you want to sell in the options chain, and then just use the interface of your broker to sell to open the option. You will be credited with the amount that the option is trading at the time. If the option expires, and the share price did not put your option in the money, then you will actually be able to take that out as cash.

Breakeven Price

Breakeven price is important to note when selling options. If the share price has not gone above the breakeven price, nobody is going to exercise the option. To take a simple example, if the share price is $100 and it costs $2 to buy the option (per-share), then the breakeven price for a call option is $102. So, the stock price has to rise above $102 to make it worth it to a buyer to exercise the option.

For a put option, subtract the price paid for the option to get the breakeven price. For our $100 stock, if a put option costs $2, then the breakeven price is $100- $2 = $98.

Buying an Option Back

One strategy used by traders who sell options is to reduce the risk of having the option exercised, they will buy the option back before it expires. This will reduce your overall profit, but eliminate the risk that a sudden price movement will put the option in the money (past breakeven) and it will be exercised. Remember that if a call option is exercised, you will be required to sell 100 shares of stock at the strike price. If a put option is exercised, you will be required to buy 100 shares of stock at the strike price. The key to this strategy is time decay. So, if you sell an option for $2 a share or $200, if it is out of the money as it nears expiration, it will be worth pennies on the dollar. So, you can buy it back without losing too much income. In the event, an option goes in the money and it looks like it is not going to move again in your favor, you can always take a slight loss and buy it back to avoid having to sell the shares.

Protected Puts

Another strategy is to sell put options, and if you are only a level 1 or level 2 traders, you can sell a protected put. However, this requires tying up a large amount of capital. To sell a protected put, you must have enough money in your account in the form of cash to buy 100 shares of the stock in the event the option is exercised. While this could be a way to earn a regular income, it requires a lot of money in proportion to small earnings, and there are better ways to earn money.

Debit Spreads

Now let's consider one of the most popular ways to earn money from selling options that don't involve having to own the shares of stock or putting up large amounts of cash. This is done using so-called bull and bears spreads or put and calls spreads. We will use the latter terminology.

A spread involves buying and selling two options at the same time. With a credit spread, it is a form of earning income. With a debit spread, you are essentially trading options but reducing the risk. So, let's look at that first.

Consider a call debit spread. With a call debit spread, you will buy an option at a lower strike price, and then sell an option at a higher strike price. The reason that traders do this is that you lower your risk by selling an option at a higher strike price. So, if the lower strike price option expires out of the money and proves to be a losing trade, you still have the premium you received by selling the option with the higher strike price. So, you will lose a lower amount of money than you would have only buying a single call option. This type of trade is entered simultaneously; that is, you buy and sell the 2 call options in a single trade, called a call debit spread. A trader can buy a call option that is in the money, to earn higher profits, and then sell a cheap out of the money call option to mitigate the risk. This strategy is used when you expect the stock price to rise.

You can also invest in a put debit spread. In this case, you buy an in the money put option with a higher strike price, and then mitigate your risk by selling an out of the money put option with a lower strike price. You use this strategy when you expect the stock price to drop.

Note that to trade spreads, you must be a level 3 options trader.

Selling Naked Put Options

A simpler trading method is to simply sell one option without buying another one to mitigate risk. Professional traders prefer this method, but you have to open a margin account to do it. This will require a cash deposit of $2,500. You will also have to deposit some collateral cash, and the requirements are higher than what is required for a credit spread. However, it is far less than what is required for a protected put, a small fraction of the money in fact.

Professional traders consider selling naked put options to be a low-risk strategy. Financial advisors are going to tell you differently, but the reality is they don't know what they are talking about. If you sell out of the money put options–while carefully studying the stocks and macroeconomic situation–it is actually a simple matter to earn profits most of the time. Remember that financial advisors are motivated to get you to invest in mutual funds and other products, so they don't like the competition. Second, the buyback strategy is used by professional options traders when selling naked put options. That means you have to be paying close attention to your trades, and then be ready to buy back any options that go in the money. When you buy back an option that you have sold, your obligations are removed.

Each broker will have a formula that determines the amount of cash you must put up as collateral. Check with your specific broker to learn the details. So, the process of selling naked put options involves depositing enough cash to cover the collateral requirements, then finding the option with the strike price that you want to sell. Brokers will tell you the probability of profit for each strike price. Professional options traders recommend selling put options with a probability of profit of 70% or higher. So, think about the number—over two years if you sell 100 put options, that means 70 of them will earn profits, and 30 of them would not. That doesn't necessarily mean you would lose money. If you are on top of things, you would be buying back the 30 options that were losing trades, not waiting to the last minute.

To sell naked options, you must be a level 4 trader.

You can also sell naked call options. The principles are the same, but when you sell naked put options, you are going to be doing so, expecting the stock price to stay above the strike price of your option. So, you are going to sell naked put options when you are neutral or bullish on the stock. For naked call options, you will sell a naked call option when you expect the stock price to be neutral or drop, so it will remain below the strike price. Then, you sell naked call options when you are bearish.

It is possible to make a high income, on the order of $500,000 to $1 million or more a year, selling naked options. But it is not without risk, so be sure to get some trading experience and do a lot of studies before you embark on a career selling options. But again, remember that most professional traders sell either naked put options or iron condors.

Chapter 4: Other Options Strategies

W̶e are now going to leave the world of selling options and go back to the one that most people are interested in, which is the world of trading options. Here, we are going to have a look at strategies that can be used to increase the odds of profits when trading options. In reality, some of these strategies involve buying and selling options at the same time. Keep in mind that these techniques will require a higher-level designation from your broker. So, it might not be something you can use right away if you are a beginner.

Selling Covered Calls Against LEAPS and Other Strategies

A LEAP is a long-term option, which is an option that expires at a date that is two years in the future. They are regular options otherwise, but you can do some interesting things with LEAPS. Because the expiration date is so far away, they cost a lot more. Looking at Apple, call options with a $195 strike price that expires in two years are selling for $28.28 (for a total price of $2,828). While that seems expensive, consider that 100 shares of Apple would cost $19,422 at the time of writing.

If you buy in the money LEAPS, then you can use them to sell covered calls. This is an interesting strategy that lets you earn premium income without having actually to buy the shares of stock.

LEAPS can also be used for other investing strategies. If at some point during those two-years, the share price rose to $200, we could exercise the option and buy the shares at $190, saving $10 a share. Also, at the same time, we could have been selling covered calls against the LEAPS.

Buying Put Options as Insurance

A put option gives you the right to sell shares of stock at a certain price. Suppose that you wanted to ensure your investment in Apple stock, and you had purchased 100 shares at $191 a share, for a total investment of $19,000. You are worried that the share price is going to drop and so you could buy a put option as a kind of insurance. Looking ahead, you see a put option with a $190 strike price for $4.10. So, you spend $410 and buy the put option.

Should the price of Apple shares suddenly tumble, you could exercise your right under the put option to dispose of your shares by selling at the strike price to minimize your losses. Suppose you wake up one morning and the share price has dropped to $170 for some reason. Had you not bought the option, you could have tried to get rid of your shares now and take a loss of $21 a share. But, since you bought the put option, you can sell your shares for $190 a share. That is a $1 loss since you purchased the shares at $191. So, your total loss would be $5.10 a share, but that is still less than the loss of $21 a share that you would have suffered selling the shares on the market at the $170 price. When investors buy stock and a put at the same time, it is called a married put.

Spreads

Spreads involve buying and selling options simultaneously. This is a more complicated options strategy that is only used by advanced traders. You will have to get a high-level designation with your brokerage in order to use this type of strategy. We won't go into details because these methods are beyond the scope of junior options traders, but we will briefly mention some of the more popular methods so that you can have some awareness.

One of the interesting things about spreads is they can be used by level 3 traders to earn a regular income from options. If you think the price of a stock is going to stay the same or rise, you sell a put credit spread. You sell a higher-priced option and buy a lower-priced option at the same time. The difference in option prices is your profit. There is a chance of loss if the price drops to the strike price of the puts (and you could get assigned if it goes below the strike price of the put option you sold). You can buy back the spread, in that case, to avoid getting assigned.

If you think that the price of a stock is going to drop, you can sell to open a credit spread, the difference in price is your profit, and losses are capped.

We can also consider more complicated spreads.

For example, you can use a diagonal spread with calls. This is done in such a way that you earn more from selling the call than you spend on buying the call for a considerable strike amount, and so you get a net credit to your account.

Spreads can become quite complicated, and there are many different types of spreads. If a trader thinks that the price of a stock will only go up a small amount, they can do a bull call spread. Profit and loss are capped in this case. The two options would have the same expiration date.

You seek to profit if the underlying stock drops in price. This can also be done by using two put options.

Spreads can be combined in more complicated ways. An iron butterfly combines a bear call spread with a bear put spread. The purpose of doing this is to generate steady income while minimizing the risk of loss.

An iron condor uses a put spread, and a call spread together. It involves selling both sides (calls and puts).

Iron Butterfly

An iron butterfly is another strategy to use if you think the stock price will stay within a certain range.

The strategy is to get as close to the money as possible. We will call the strike priced used the central strike. Then you set a differential price we will call x.

Like an iron condor, the profit from an iron butterfly is fixed at the net credit when you sell to open. This is given by the sum of the premiums earned from selling the money call and put, minus the prices paid for the out of the money options.

The maximum loss is the strike price of the purchased call–strike price of the sold put–total premium.

Chapter 5: Avoiding Common Pitfalls in Options Trading

All successful options traders go through a learning curve before they start profiting consistently. Some of them put in an all-out effort to learn by spending countless hours reading on the topic or by watching video tutorials. Others learn at a more leisurely pace and once they get a grip of the basics, they lean more towards learning from their own experience. Irrespective of the type of learner you are, one way to cut short that learning curve is by learning from the mistakes of others.

This lists out six of the most common mistakes made by inexperienced traders that can be easily avoided.

1. Buying Naked Options without Hedging

This is one of the most fundamental mistakes made by amateur options traders and is also one of the costliest ones that could make them go broke in no time.

Buying naked options means buying options without any protective trades to cover your investment if the underlying security moves against your expectations and hurts your trade.

Here is a typical example:

A trader strongly feels a particular stock will go up in the short term and assumes he can make a huge profit by buying a few call options and therefore goes ahead with the purchase. The trader knows if the underlying stock's price were to rise as expected, the potential upside on the profits would be unlimited, whereas, if it were to go down, the maximum loss would be curtailed to just the amount invested for purchasing the call options.

In theory, the trader's assumption is right and it may so happen that this one particular trade may pay off. However, in reality, it is equally possible the stock would not move as per expectations, or may even fall. If the latter happens, the call options' prices would start falling rapidly and may never recover, thereby causing major losses to that trader.

It is almost impossible to predict the short-term movement of a stock accurately every time and the trader who consistently keeps buying naked options hoping to get lucky is far more likely to lose much more than what he/she gains in the long term.

For a person to make a profit after buying a naked option, the following things should fall in place:

1. The trader should predict the direction of the underlying stock's movement correctly.

2. The directional movement of the stock price should be quick enough so that the position can be closed before its gains get overrun by time-decay.

3. The rise in the option's premium price should also compensate for any potential drop in implied volatility from the time the option was purchased.

4. The trader should exit the trade at the right time before a reversal of the stock movement happens.

Needless to say, it is impractical to expect everything to fall in place simultaneously always and that is why naked-options traders often end up losing money even when they correctly guess the direction of the underlying stock's movement.

Having said all this, many such traders often think they would fare better the next time after a botched trade and rinse and repeat their actions till they reach a point where they would have lost most of their capital and are forced to quit trading altogether.

My advice to you – never buy naked options (unless it is part of a larger strategy to hedge some position) because it's simply not worth the risk.

Note: While buying naked-options has only finite risk limited to the price of the premium paid, selling of naked-options has unlimited risk and has to be avoided too, unless hedged properly.

2. Underestimating Time-Decay

A second major mistake of inexperienced traders is underestimating time-decay.

Time-decay is your worst enemy if you are an option buyer and you don't get a chance to exit your trade quickly enough.

If you are a call options buyer, you will notice that sometimes, even when your underlying stock's price is increasing every day, your call option's price still doesn't rise or even falls. Alternately, if you are a put options buyer, you sometimes notice that your put option's price doesn't increase despite a fall in the price of the underlying stock. Both these situations can be confusing to somebody new to options trading.

The above problems occur when the rate of increase/decrease in the underlying stock's price is just not enough to outstrip the rate at which the option's time-value is eroding every day.

Therefore, any trading strategy deployed by an options trader should ideally have a method of countering/minimizing the effect of time-decay, or should make time-decay work in its favor, to ensure a profitable trade.

The spread based strategies do exactly that.

3. Buying Options with High Implied Volatility

Buying options in times of high volatility is yet another common mistake.

During times of high volatility, option premiums can get ridiculously overpriced and at such times, if an options trader buys options, even if the stock moves sharply in line with the trader's expectation, a large drop in the implied volatility would result in the option prices falling by a fair amount, resulting in losses to the buyer.

A particular situation I remember happened the day the results of the 'Brexit' referendum came through in 2016. The Nifty index reacting to the result (like most other global indices such as the Nasdaq 100) fell very sharply and the volatility index (VIX) jumped up by over 30%. The options premium for all Nifty options had become ludicrously high that day. However, this rise in volatility was only because of the market's knee-jerk reaction to an unexpected result and just a couple of days later, the market stabilized and started rising again; the VIX fell sharply and also brought down option premium prices accordingly.

Option traders who bought options at the time VIX was high, would have realized their mistake a day or two later when the option prices came down, causing them substantial losses because the volatility started to get back to normal figures.

4. Not Cutting Losses on Time

There is apparently a famous saying among the folks on Wall Street - "Cut your losses short and let your winners run."

Even the most experienced options traders will make a bad trade once in a while. However, what differentiates them from a novice is that they know when to concede defeat and cut their losses. Amateurs hold on to losing trades in the hope they'll bounce back and eventually end up losing a larger chunk of their capital. The experienced traders, who know when to concede defeat, pull out early and reinvest the capital elsewhere.

Cutting losses in time is crucial, especially when you trade a directional strategy and make a wrong call. The practical thing to do is to exit a losing position if it moves against expectation and erodes more than 2-3% of your total capital.

If you are a trader who strictly uses spread-based strategies, your losses will always be far more limited whenever you make a wrong call. Nevertheless, irrespective of the strategy used, when it becomes evident that the probability of profiting from a trade is too less for whatsoever reason, it is prudent to cut losses and reinvest in a different position that has a greater chance of success rather than simply crossing your fingers or appealing to a higher power.

5. Keeping Too Many Eggs in the Same Basket

The experienced hands always know that once in a while, they will lose a trade. They also know that they should never bet too much on a single trade, which could considerably erode their capital were it to go wrong.

Professionals spread their risk across different trades and keep a maximum exposure of not more than 4-5% of their total available capital in a single trade for this very reason.

Therefore, if you have a total capital of $10,000, do not enter any single trade that has a risk of losing more than $500 in the worst-case scenario. Following such a practice will ensure the occasional loss is something you can absorb without seriously eroding your cash reserve. Fail to follow this rule and you may have the misfortune of seeing many months of profits wiped out by one losing trade.

6. Using Brokers Who Charge High Brokerages

A penny saved is a penny earned!

When I first entered the stock market many years ago, I didn't pay much attention to the brokerage I was paying. After all, the trading services I received were from one of the largest and most reputed banks in the country, and the brokerage charged by my provider wasn't very different from that of other banks that provided similar services.

Over the years, many discount brokerage firms started flourishing that charge considerably less, but I had not bothered changing my broker since I was used to the old one.

It was only when I quantified the differences that I realized having a low-cost broker made a huge difference.

If you are somebody who trades in the Indian Stock markets, check the table below for a quantified break-up of how brokerage charges can eat into your earnings over a year if you choose the wrong broker. The regular broker in the table below is the bank whose trading services I had been using and the discount broker is the one I use now. For the record, the former is also India's third-largest bank in the private sector and the latter is the most respected discount broker house in the country.

	Regular Broker	Discount Broker
Brokerage charged per options trade	₹ 300	₹ 20
Cost of entering any directional spread and exiting the position before expiry	₹ 1,200	₹ 80
Cost of entering an Iron Condor and taking it to expiry	₹ 1,200	₹ 80
Percentage of profits surrendered as brokerage for a typical Iron-Condor on Nifty index (Considering profit of ₹ 3300 for a trade with 70% winning probability)	36.36%	2.42%

Comparison of brokerages : Regular Broker versus Discount Broker

It is obvious from the table above that using a low-cost broker makes a huge difference, especially when trading a strategy such as the Iron Condor (a relatively low-yield but high-probability strategy).

Also, it is not just the brokerage that burns a hole in your pocket; the annual maintenance fee is also higher for a regular broker and all these costs will make a huge difference in the long run.

Irrespective of which part of the world you trade from, always opt for a broker that provides the lowest possible brokerage because this will make a difference in the long term. Do a quantitative comparison using a table (something similar to the one I used above) and that would make it easier to decide who you should go with.

Note for India-based Traders: If you are a trader based in India or if you trade in the Indian Stock markets, I would strongly suggest using Zerodha, which has been consistently rated the best discount broker in the country. I have been using their services for the past couple of years and have found them to be particularly good. Their brokerage rates are among the best in the country, and on top of that, they provide excellent support when needed, and also maintain an exhaustive knowledge-base of articles. Lastly, their trading portal is very user friendly and therefore, placing an order is quick and hassle-free.

Chapter 6: The Most Common Questions about Trading

1. Can you live on trading?

Yes, just as you can live from medicine, from being a teacher, from being an architect, engineer, or lawyer. You require the same weapons: education, training, practice, guidance, discipline, perseverance, and a lot of determination to be a great professional in your field. Trading is no different. Perhaps many people have been wrong to think that when opening an account in a broker, funding their accounts, and starting trading means having the results to live from trading in less than what a rooster sings and being millionaires. Very wrong!!! It's like pretending to be a surgeon overnight. If you can live from trading, the question is, do you have what it takes to do it and achieve it?

2. What do I do to start trading?

The first and most important thing is to educate yourself about what trading is and how to do it effectively. Start by knowing the nature of trading, what it is about, how you win, who participates, how is the market that has been chosen, etc., are some of the things you should keep in mind. Don't get to war empty-handed. Go prepared. How? Find someone to inspire you, to teach these things, to guide you, invest money and time in your education. There are many online trading schools, and you can be overwhelmed at first by searching, but choose the one that has a simple system, that its philosophy resonates with you, and that has your feet set on the ground. Avoid those that promote phrases like "fast millionaire trading in the Stock Exchange," "trading is straightforward," etc. You have to be realistic, and a school that tells you from the beginning what is trading, how it works, how it is earned, how it is lost and that it is not as easy as many want to make it believe in profiting, is a school that is worth considering.

3. When will I start seeing results?

When you have firmly rooted in a simple trading system, faithfully and disciplined, fulfilling your trading plan and adequately managing the risk-benefit, paradoxically, you will also begin to see the results when you detach yourself from the results and focus on the process. The process of trading involves the observation and reflection of our performance, the emotions experienced, the most frequent mistakes and annihilation, the analysis of the logbook, and the correction of the things that you can change and improve. You will begin to see results when, in addition to all these things, you continue working on your mind without giving up.

4. How much money can I start trading, and what broker should I use?

It depends on each broker and the instrument you use. If you want to trade stock options in Thinkorswim, for example, you will need at least $ 2,000 to access the options. If you're going to trade with stocks, you will need $ 25,000. With the other brokers, it will be different. On the website of the brokers are the most frequent questions and customer service that can take you from all doubts regarding minimum money to start, documents such as funds and how to remove, etc. Find the broker that is regulated, that has a good reputation that other people are using and tell you about their experience.

5. How much money per month can I generate by trading?

The one that allows you the size of your account and the amount you are going to invest per operation, as long as you have the capabilities required to make money consistently. This brings us to question # 1. It's that easy.

6. How to achieve consistency?

Consistency is achieved by having disciplined behaviors and constant actions. That is if I have planned trading that tells me what an opportunity looks like, where to go, where to place the stop, how to manage and how to manage risk, and do it over and over again, then I'll have consistent results. But, if you change the policy, each has a stop, or every time you have a losing streak, then you will go into an endless loop in which an emotional and impatient trader will modify, or change it again and again, the plan and the results will be different. This is what happens to 95% who lose money doing trading; there is no clear, defined, and precise plan to follow consistently, disciplined, and with a lot of confidence.

7. What is the best strategy or trading system?

The one that is simple to understand, that you can even explain it to a child and the child understands it. Stay away from those systems that require more than five different indicators, where your attention gets away from price action and do not have proper management of risk-benefit. The best strategy or system is simple, clear, proven (functional), and above all, fits your personality and type of trader.

The method of a particular trader may not be the system that suits you; for that reason, you must define what type of trader you are: whether you are scalper, intraday or swing, and of course, your risk tolerance (conservative or risky). These are just a few things to consider when choosing a trading system.

8. I have lost much of my capital; what do I do?

If you have lost a large part of your capital, it is because you do not have a clear, defined, and proven trading plan, there are no consistent behaviors that lead to consistent results; emotions dominate you, and there is also no proper risk-benefit management. In that sentence is the answer to this question. What you should do is simple: make a clear trading plan with a clear and straightforward strategy, try it in a demo, manage risk-benefit properly, trust 100% in your plan, work on your emotions being aware of them before, during and after of operations, record, and evaluate to be able to learn from your failures.

If the results are positive, return to real account and repeat the process focusing your attention on the emotions you experience and your reactions.

9. What actions do you recommend operating to start?

I recommend trading stocks that do not have a widespread, that are not very volatile and offer economic contracts near ITM. These are terms that you may not understand if you are starting. Once you know what the ideal requirements are, go to the Finviz map of actions and look for the best-known actions in each sector, write them down, go to your platform and look at their contract and spread grid, so you are choosing and removing from the list until having your ideal portfolio of at least 6 shares.

10. I have no time to trading regularly, what are my options?

You can choose to do swing trading. The swing will allow you to open an operation today and close it several days later. Some brokers have mobile applications that allow you to monitor operations from your cell phone. If the situation is that you cannot trade in the morning, you can choose to make a trading plan for the afternoon hours, and it will work the same.

Chapter 7: Introduction to Spreads

Positions that are composed of at least two of the same options that have limited risks, but also limited gains, are called Spread strategies. These strategies can be horizontal, vertical, diagonal and box range. Vertical ranges include purchase and sale of an equal number of the same options with the same maturity date.

Depending on whether you bind on expectations of price change of the underlying assets or the level of its volatility, the spreads can be bull, bear, and wingspreads, and each one of them can be achieved by the call and put options. Each spread must be made "in a package."

The horizontal spread represents the investment strategy being carried out simultaneously by taking long and short positions in the same type of option on the same underlying assets at the same time of maturity but with different exercise prices. Depending on which options are used in the preparation of the horizontal range, we can see the difference between:

Bull Call Spread

Bull Put Spread

Bear Call Spread

Bear put Spread

Bull Call/Bear Put Spread

A spread is a difference between prices. Here, the spread will be on the strike prices of two sets of options. As with the straddles and strangles, this will require more than one piece. This involves buying and selling in the same trade, but we will limit the risk in the option writing with this strategy. I will give you an example here of a bull call spread, but the same applies (using the converse) for bear puts.

Winning outcome of bull spread is related to the increase in the price of the underlying assets, while the success of the bear spread is the expected substantial decrease in prices.

Bulls call spread is assembled in a way to buy a call option of underlying assets with a series of excellent prices and to sell the call options on the same property but with a higher strike price. The success of this type of spread depends on the increase in asset prices and the fall in prices, which will cause a loss. In this way, possible gains and losses are limited.

The preparation of the strategy of a bull put spread starts from the same position as for the various strike prices, so the bull call spread consists of purchasing put options with a lower price and a put option with a higher cost. In the case that the price increases, one will achieve limited gains, while the price drop will cause limited losses. A great price depends on the price of the put option. An investor who has a strategy bull put spread has a range of credit because he earned money on the difference in price. The investor buys an option at a lower price but sells another option at a high price. That's why we talk about credit range. If prices rose above most strike prices, investors with bulls put spreads strategies will achieve the greatest profits. But in a case of price drops below the lowest strike prices, this spreads strategies will achieve a limited loss of premiums.

Bear Put Spread is a combination of purchasing put options on certain underlying assets with the higher strike price, as well as drawing up a put option on the same property with a number of strike prices. This strategy gain is realized in the event of falling prices since the investor has the bear's expectations. Maximum height loss and gain are limited. As in the above ranges, the price of the put option depends on a strike price, and the option increases with the strike price. Since the put option makes a profit in the case of prices drop, profits will be higher if the strike price is higher. This is why the bear put spread is a debit range. Specifically, the investor loses the difference between the price at which he buys and sells options. Given that the maximum loss is limited, the worst that can happen is that, at the moment of maturity, the share price is to be above the most of the strike prices. In this case, both of the put options are worthless and the loss is limited to the amount of the premium.

As always, this trade can be reversed to deal with falling prices. It can also be implemented in both directions with both puts and calls. You have to determine the entry point based on the current price and how much you are willing to lose, your expected direction of the stock, and the possible profit, which is capped.

Butterflies

This one is even more complicated, and it requires three components. The basic idea is to buy one low, in-the-money call, selling two at-the-money calls and finally buying a high, out-of-the-money call. This is a strategy for when you expect the market to move sideways, for the highest profit is in the middle and you can maintain a profit within a range. As with most of these strategies involving more than one component, the risk and reward are both limited.

The profit is highest when the spot price is equal to the two written calls. You keep the premium for both written (short) calls, but lose the premiums paid on the two purchased (long) calls. The higher long call is going to cost much less than the short call premiums, as it is far out-of-the-money, but the lower long call is going to cost more since it is either in-the-money or at least closer to being so. The risk is capped at the premiums paid for the long calls. If the underlying is below the lower strike or above the higher strike on your longs, you will incur the maximum loss. From that, you can easily see this strategy is for range trading. You can make big spreads, but keep in mind the profits will be based on how far into the money you are. You can make this more complicated, but you must retain symmetry. Notice that the long and short positions have equal numbers of shares at stake and you should keep your expiration dates the same. Otherwise, you will either open yourself up to a huge risk or diminish your possible profits.

This spread is not directed to increase or to decrease the price of the underlying assets. The investor who chooses a strategy of short butterfly trading expects a significant change in the price, in any direction, regardless of whether it is rising or falling, of the underlying assets. The short butterfly spread is possible to draw up the buying and selling options. If a short butterfly is made up of put options, the trader sells one option with lower and one with the higher exercise price and buys two put options with an average exercise price. Butterfly range can be made in four different ways, which points to its complexity. This includes:

1. The Purchase of a Call Option with the Highest and Lowest Reasonable Price and the Simultaneous Sale of Two Call Options at an Average Price.

2. The Purchase of a Put Option with the Highest and Lowest Exercise Price and the Simultaneous Sale of Two Put Options with High Prices

3. The Purchase of a Call Option at the Lowest Exercise Price, and Selling Call Options at an Average Price Along with the Purchase of Put Options at the Highest Price, and Sell Put Options at an Average Exercise Price

4. The Purchase of Put Options at the Lowest Exercise Price and Selling Put Options at an Average Price with the Purchase of a Call Option at the Highest Exercise Price and Sell Call Options at an Average Exercise Prices

Condor Spread

Condor spread consists of two horizontal spreads of conflicting expectations and includes four options on the same underlying assets with the same due date. Four different exercise prices for each option show the complexity of the Condor spread.

Condor Spread with Call Options

The similarity of the condor spread with the butterfly spread is inevitable, but the difference is that in the condor spread, there are two different medium exercise prices and the butterfly spread has only one. To perform the long condor spread with the call options trader must buy a call option with a range of exercise price, sell a call option with a slightly higher exercise price, sell a call option with an even greater exercise price, and buy a call option with the highest exercise price.

Vertical Spread

The simultaneous purchase and sale, purchase or sale of options on the same underlying assets, and the same exercise price, but in different maturities, is resulting in the vertical spread. The vertical spread is referred to as the calendar spread due to the use of different maturities. We can distinguish calendar put spread and calendar call spread. These types of neutral strategies can be focused on the growth and drop in asset prices. Combining the different times of maturity in the compiling spread, the investor combines intrinsic value, and time value, of occupied positions in a particular option. In this way, in a case of the option with less time, the investor is set to its intrinsic value, while with the options with a longer time to maturity; the investor puts in the time value of options as a primary goal.

Neutral Calendar Spread

If prices rise or fall in relation to the strike price, the composer of the vertical spread is faced with limited loss. The compiler spread can achieve only limited losses. The main purpose of the assemblers of a neutral calendar spread with call options is to close before expiration of the call option with a shorter expiration time and, at the same time, to expect price stability relative to the price of the call exercise.

Bulls' Calendar Spread

These are aggressive calendar spreads that have bull's expectations, therefore, focused on the increase in share prices or other property. Bull's calendar spread is within a certain range, also neutral, it is compiled with the current market price that is below the strike price of the calendar spread. The advantages of such spread are lower initial cost and a good chance of making the profit, but with significant risk.

To the compiler of the bull calendar spread, achieved profits are required in two events. First, he will make a call option with a shorter time to maturity (short option), which should expire worthlessly. Therefore, the range and draw up options go beyond—because the money is likely to call option with a shorter time to maturity. In this way, the investor is left with a call option with a longer time to maturity (longer optional). Secondly, it is necessary to increase the prices of the underlying assets in the strike price range, after the maturity date of options. If the price increases, the investor will make a profit.

Chapter 8: Options and Leverage

As with any investment, your brokerage firm will likely offer leverage, that is, money loaned to you to be invested. While this greatly increases your ability to enter into potentially profitable positions, it obviously increases your risk as well. A quick refresher on leverage is in order, but we assume you have a good understanding of the concept, so we'll keep it brief. The reason leverage is so frequently used in all types of trading is that individual traders frequently lack the capital to make meaningful moves in the market. If your broker offers leverage of 3:1, for instance, that means that for every dollar you put in of your own money, your broker will loan you three dollars to enlarge your investment.

Of course, this money must be paid back, but because of the nature of investing, your profits will still be increased. Let's look at an example. You have found a stock that you think is attractive. You buy 100 shares at $1 per share. Your brokerage gives you leverage at 3:1, so you are able to invest $300 of their money as well. So, in total, you hold 400 shares of the stock. The stock doubles in price the next week, and you are able to sell all 400 shares for a total of $800. After you pay your broker back their $300 investment, you're left with a profit of $500. Without leverage, if you had only been able to invest your original $100, you would have been able to sell those 100 shares for $200.

Your profit with leverage is $300 greater than it would have been. This is clearly a very dramatic example for the sake of clarity, but the increased percentages in profits using leverage are very real. You can never forget, however, that the opposite is also true. If your stock in the above example had tanked, you would still be on the hook to your broker for the $300 investment that is now lost. So, instead of just losing your own $100, you would have multiplied your monetary loss by a multiple of three.

Now that we're all on the same page, we'll look at special considerations that are important when trading in options.

Options are, as we've talked about before, derivatives. Most derivatives are, by their nature, riskier than simply buying the underlying asset outright. Because of this, brokers require traders who are seeking leverage to buy options to sign a form stating that they understand the risk of using leverage in options trading. This has contributed to the reputation of options as being an especially, even unacceptably risky investment. Don't let this scare you away, though. Risk is often thought of as the "boogeyman" in investing, but let's thinks critically for a moment. If you were completely averse to risk, you'd put all of your money in T Bills, or bury it in the back yard. Risk is simply the other half of the opportunity coin.

In a way, options function as their own kind of leverage. You may not have the cash on hand to be able to buy 100 shares of some stock. The option will be much cheaper than the stock itself, so you may want to buy the option and then, when it's proven that it will be possible, use the leverage from your broker to exercise your option. With trading strategies that have as many steps as most options trades have, an example is usually helpful. Note that in these examples, we've eliminated brokerage fees for the sake of clarity.

Let's say shares of Spatulas R Us stock are trading at $40 per share. You have looked into the spatula industry and expect it to boom in the upcoming months. SRU is a leader in its industry, so you're pretty confident they will rise in price. All but $4000 of your investment capital is tied up in other ways at the moment though. So, if you were to buy the shares outright, you could only buy 100 shares. Let's look at two paths: buying outright and using an option as leverage.

In the first instance, you would buy your 100 shares. Then, just as you predicted, the spatula boom caused the price of your SRU stock to rise to $42 per share. You sell them, making a $200 profit. This is a 5% profit of your total investment. Not bad!

In the second instance, you look up the price for an SRU stock option and see that it's $50. You go ahead and buy 4 options, meaning you have the opportunity to buy 400 shares during the duration of your contract. The same boom happens, and SRU goes up to $42 per share. You exercise your option, and either by liquidating other assets or borrowing from your broker, buy those 400 shares for the $40 price you locked in when you purchased your option. You immediately sell them for the new price of $42, giving you an immediate profit of $800. Of course, you still spent $200 on options in the first place, so your real profit is $600. That might not sound like a shockingly big difference, but look at the percentages! Your profit, in this instance, is 15% of the original investment.

Of course, there is the possibility that the spatula boom you foresaw does not actually happen. Let's take a look at what happens in the above situations when you are wrong. (We are going to assume that you're not a terrible trader and have your stop losses in place. You do, right?)

Alright, let's say you're sitting there, the proud owner of 100 SRU shares that you paid your $4000 for. The stock price drops, and you dump the stocks at $36 (a 10% drop, which is a common point at which to set your stop loss). You've realized a loss of $400, or 10% of your investment.

In the example where you bought the options instead of the stock outright, your investment was only $200. You simply decide not to exercise the option when you see that the stock is dropping. You do lose the money you paid for the premiums, but your total loss is only 5% of what you would have invested had you exercised the option.

Now let's look at how leverage can stack up with the natural leveraging effect of options. As you've seen, leverage can be used to exercise an option that you might not have the capital to otherwise. But what about using leverage to purchase the option itself? Many experts avoid this for any reason because the risk that the option will never pay off is just too high. That's a determination you'll have to make for yourself. When you do, make sure that you are doing the math correctly and clearly, and know what your potential gains and losses are on the deal before you enter into the position. Let's look at an example of what the above situation would have looked like had you used leverage to purchase the options.

First, let's look at the sunnier prospect: you were right about the spatula industry, and the stock jumps up. Let's say your broker offered leverage at a rate of 3:1.

You decide that with that rate, you can buy many more options. You purchase 16 options instead of 4, but your initial input is still only $200 because your brokerage supplies the other $600 in the form of leverage. The stock rises as before, you exercise your options, and then immediately sell the shares for a profit of $2 per share. That nets you $3200! After subtracting the $600 you have to pay back to your broker, you're still left with $2600, a whopping 1300% increase on your initial outlay of $200.

Now let's look at what happens if the spatula boom does not pan out and you don't end up exercising any of these options. Your total loss is $800, your $200 plus the $600 you have to pay your broker back. That's a loss of four times as much just buying the smaller amount of options and having them not work out, and twice as much of a loss as buying the stock outright (assuming you don't let your losses run out of control.)

You will rarely have to calculate the delta of an option on your own anymore because almost every investing software or website will do it for you. It's still valuable to know what it is because you will see it from time to time. If an option has a delta value of 1 which means that the option and underlying asset are moving in lock-step, a delta value of 0 means that they are moving independently of one another. The delta value is an important value indicator because it indicates whether an option is "in the money," "at the money," or "out of the money." These phrases mean whether the option's strike prices are above, even to, or below the current price of the underlying stock. For put options, the same phrases are used, but they indicate negative movement rather than positive.

Intrinsic Value

The intrinsic value of an option is the difference between the asset price and the strike price. For a call option, it is calculated by subtracting the stock price from the strike price. For put options, it is the opposite. An intrinsic value of zero indicates that the difference calculated in these equations is negative.

Extrinsic Value

This is also known as the "time value" of an option. It is the difference between the market value, i.e., what the market is willing to pay for the option, and the intrinsic value. In the case of a call option, if the current market price is below the strike price, then the only value the option has is its extrinsic value. For put options, it is the opposite. The time before the expiration date is the main factor determining extrinsic value. The more time there is before an option expires, the more time there is for it to move in a profitable direction, so this makes sense. An option that is out of the money (the current stock price is below the strike price in the case of call options, above the strike price for puts) with an expiration date several months away is going to have a higher extrinsic value than one that expires in a few days.

The other main factor in calculating extrinsic value is the volatility of the underlying asset. The more implied volatility the asset has, the higher the extrinsic value will be. This will shift over the life of the option as the market shifts. Just as buying an option at a low price when you suspect the price will rise is the goal of successful options trading, so is buying one with low volatility that you expect to rise.

Chapter 9: Options Trading Mistakes to Avoid

O
ption trading can be challenging to master, and you may find
yourself going through a frustrating period of trial and error in
an attempt to get it right. This is especially likely if you are
completely new to options trading, and attempt to view it from the eyes of regular
stock market trading. Options trading follow its unique set of rules, and not being
conversant with these rules is what can lead you to make some time consuming
and costly mistakes.

To save you time, these are the mistakes you are likely to make before getting it right. With this information, you can avoid these mistakes and fast track successful options trading.

Mistake #1 – Applying One Strategy in Every Situation

Different market conditions require differing unique approaches. Sometimes, an options trader will apply the only strategy he knows to every option purchase he makes. This can lead to loss of money and disaster on your portfolio. Buying spreads should be considered as a solution to this problem, and they will fix the mistake. Buying spreads allow you to trade effectively in a range of market conditions. A spread means that you purchase a myriad of options and adopt different strategies to suit these options. In a way, you could say that you are effectively spreading your risk. When you buy several spreads, you adopt a 'long spread' position.

The long spread position has two options – a high-cost option which is bought and a low-cost option which is sold. These options will have some conditions for security, expiration, and type of options, which will make it easier to choose the strategy. You can then evaluate the values to make a decision as to when to hold on to your options, or when to sell them. The only thing to watch out for is that using a spread approach may lead to multiple options traded that incur multiple commissions, which may mean higher expenses.

Mistake #2 –Buying Out Of the Money Call Options From the Onset

Most people attempt new ways to invest with a little trepidation because they want to avoid loss, especially a large loss. For that reason, when some opt for options trading, they start with buying call options, as this allows for "testing the waters." It allows for buying low and selling high. Unfortunately, this method is not consistent in the long run and may lead to losing money. Therefore, one needs to consider at least one other strategy to go hand in hand with call options when purchasing. The reason for this is when you buy options, you need to be right about the direction of the move and the timing. A mistake on either of these factors may result in completely losing the option premium paid.

Mistake #3 – Breaking Your Own Rules

When you start trading and you move into your rhythm, you are likely to create specific rules to follow, so as to avoid compromising or loss leading situations in the future. These rules may include 'never selling in the money options' or 'never buying out of the money options.'

When you are faced with an option trade that is going against you, you will definitely be tempted to break all your own rules. This happens when you give in to panic and start reasoning from your emotions, rather than from your options plan. Although when trading in the stock market, you can justify changing your own rules by "doubling up to catch up" for example, this is not possible in the options trading setting.

To evaluate your position before you do something irrational, look at the situation and ask yourself whether you would have made the same move you are now contemplating when you first opened your options. If your answer is a resounding no, do not break your own rules. Consider an alternative game plan.

Mistake #4 – Not Planning Your Exit

It is important to remember that options are decaying assets, and the rate of decay quickly accelerates as the expiration date approaches. In any type of investment you make, you need to have an exit plan in case things go awry. This is also very applicable if things appear to be going well with your options. For options trading, this plan should include your upside exit point and your downside exit point, and your proposed timeframe to complete your exit. As much as possible, you should avoid giving in to greed, particularly if it seems like the options are within your upside exit point as you may be tempted to hold on to them in the hope of gaining more profit.

A plan will stop you from leaving your option too early due to panic, which would mean that you miss out on possible high returns. It will also help you make the right decision when you are experiencing an upswing, as holding on for too long can suddenly lead to extreme loss. An exit plan helps you conceptualize your worst-case scenario on the downside and how it is; you would deal with it once it occurs. It also helps you set upside goals that establish your position for when you want to take your profits and move on.

Options trading requires serious scenario concentration and planning, and should not be driven by emotions. As with any investment, when you purchase options, you should keep in mind that there always exists the possibility that you will completely lose your investment. This is why it is important to have a plan ready.

Mistake #5 – Trading Illiquid Options

A quote options form the market will have a different bid price and ask price. They do not show the actual value of the option, as the value is somewhere in the middle of the bid and ask. The distance between the bid and ask prices depends on the options liquidity.

At-the-money and near-the-money options which have near term expiration are usually the most liquid, meaning that if the need arises, they can quickly be converted to cash. As your strike price moves further from the at the money strike price or expiration date goes further into the future, the options are less liquid.

There is the point in trading in options that cannot be easily liquidated when the need arises. Illiquid options can lose you a lot of money as if you are trying to save them suddenly, their prices can drop significantly. You should focus on purchasing liquid options that have an active number of buyers and sellers.

73

Illiquid options are most prevalent with smaller stocks, causing the bid and ask prices to get artificially wide.

Mistake #6 – Wasting Time When Buying Back Stock Options

You should be ready and willing to buy back stock options you may have sold. This can help you save on commission charges and make a little more profit from the trade. You could also consider buying back your options immediately if you are able to keep 80% or more of your initial gain.

Take, for example, you had a contract that spans a period of four months. Within the second month, you are lucky and have already realized an excellent profit. Rather than waiting, you should see your stock options to cash in on your profit, and immediately reinvest your 'principal' in some more of the same options. It could be possible that you will get more profit before your contract end date comes up again.

Mistake #7 – Not Understanding Implied Volatility

You must take time to understand the intricacies of option pricing and volatility. Implied volatility helps you gauge whether an option is cheap or expensive based on past price action in the underlying stock.

If you understand implied volatility, you can consistently make money when trading options. The less volatile an option is, the more liquid it becomes, and the easier it is to sell your options so that you can realize your profits.

Mistake #8 – Ignoring Powerful Compounded Small Gains

The most successful options traders will have steady profits as they use a range of strategies and set goals like attaining a monthly gain from 2-4%. Options traders should avoid taking extreme risks, as you could be up 100% in one month, and then down 70% in the next month. Although there is room for speculation, you should pick your options spots carefully.

It is far better to put together the small profits which can be gained from a spread than to hold out in the hope that you will make one big return from a single option. The gains from a range of options are likely to add up and offer more than what one option could provide in the long run.

Mistake #9 – Not Understanding Time Decay

Options can easily be a wasting asset. A trader needs to keep in mind the price of an option until the time of expiration. So, purchasing puts or calls outright with the underlying stock moving in your direction slowly may means the option does not gain in value. Also, the nearer an option gets to its expiry date, the more important it becomes to sell that option so that you can avoid losing your investment.

Mistake #10–Not Paying Attention to Market Moving Events

If you create an options trade based on a quiet market condition, you will profit as long as the underlying assets stay docile. You need to keep an eye out for market-moving events that might affect your stock during the time frame of your trade. An earnings release could increase volatility and change market conditions, putting a stop could change your quiet time plan.

Your strategy should be able to accommodate such changes and as an options trader. You should be aware of what is occurring in a range of financial markets, whether or not you believe that you will be affected.

Chapter 10: Options Trading Account

Your trading account is where all options trading activities will be done. Basically, an options trading account is a system or platform used by an investor to purchase and buy financial securities such as stocks, indexes, and many others. The trading account is held by the brokerage firm and used to manage trading activities on your behalf. With an online trading account, you can hold cash, stocks, and other type of securities.

Technology has made it easy for managing trading accounts. To start using your trading account, you must first of all fund it. Many people think they can use an account from a friend to fund their options trading. Well, that is not allowed. Your bank account will be connected to the trading account. Through bank wire or transfer, you can transfer funds into the brokerage account through your savings or checking accounts.

Another factor to consider is a tax. Your trading account can be taxable or tax-deferred like a 401 (k). You can also decide if your trading account will be taxable or simply a non-retirement account. You can choose to open an individual account or brokerage account for your business to trade. These are just forms of trading account, but there are two main types based on their functionality: margin and cash trading account.

Margin vs. Cash Trading Account

Margin Trading Account: A margin account is simply a brokerage account that provides you with a line of credit to buy options, stocks, and other securities. Are you planning on using leverage for your trading? Through a margin trading account, you can borrow money to buy stocks or options. This gives you a form of leverage if you don't have cash at hand to purchase securities.

What you need to know about the margin trading account is that all margins come with an interest. All the money borrowed to you for trading has an interest associated with it. That means for each that trade you are successful with; the brokerage account has to deduct taxes, fees and interests used in purchasing the securities.

The typical rate is 2% over the prime interest rate. An Intraday Margin Account, for instance, works on a 4:1 leverage ratio. That means for every amount of equity that you have, you will be granted access to credit four (4) times that amount. Let's say that you have a cash amount of $ 1,000 through an intra-margin account you can borrow as much as $ 4,000 for your trading activities.

Cash Trading Account: A trading account deals with only cash. There is no line of credits for you to borrow the securities you deem feasible for you. All trading transactions in your account will be done via the cash you have transferred into the trading account via your savings or checking bank account. This account means you have no form of leverage for all trading decisions.

For instance, when you placed $1,000 into your cash trading account, the only money available for you to spend in buying and trading securities will be that $1,000.00. If you don't close any position in your trading account, you will not have any line of credit to provide you with purchasing power. The settlement date for cash accounts varies, but they can be as short as the day of the transaction and the following one.

Steps to Open a Trading Account

1. Providing Personal Information

To open a trading account, the brokerage firm will require you to provide certain personal financial information. This financial information helps the broker to track, manage and handle your account. You need to be careful you provide the right details to facilitate smooth trading activities. The sign-up process for a brokerage account varies from one broker to another, but the personal information required to run the account is almost the same.

2. Providing Additional Information

The following information must be provided: Your legal name, email address, social security number, employment status, approximate annual income, and others. Some brokers want to know your experience level in trading underlying securities like stocks, index funds, and options.

Are you a registered broker-dealer? Are you managing a brokerage account on behalf of an individual or an institution? Are you a shareholder in a company assigned to manage the brokerage account for the company? All this additional information will be asked to enable the broker to tailor their services to you. A special disclosure obligation will also be provided to authenticate and protect the information provided.

3. Idle Cash Management

If you have idle cash in your brokerage account, how will it be managed? Your broker would want to know how you intend to handle or manage the account. For example, you have invested and earned $16,500 worth of money. You have decided to trade in other securities with $10,000, what would you like the idle 6,500 to do? You might want to instruct the broker to push it into interest-bearing accounts such as treasury funds, mutual funds or even the money markets.

4. Trading Account Suitability

There are various kinds of trading styles. Your broker would want to know the best way you want to handle risk and manage trading activities. It is the goal of the broker to know the customer and provide the best support and services to be successful in trading activities. Some of the trading styles can be: aggressive growth (more risk-taking in volatile securities), Simple Growth (gain money while preserving original capital), Income Risk Level (using income generate from profits for further trading) and Conservative (capital preservation and using the account of only one thing to protect existing assets).

5.   Signing Account Opening Agreement

Before the trading account is opened, the broker would ensure that you sign and approve all the information provided. You might want to check all the information provided as well as read the contract statement to know the terms, policies and conditions used by the broker in managing the trading account. Once you are done, you can then confirm to agree with the terms for the trading contract. An electronic signature, print & sign or mail & sign will be used.

CONCLUSION

Thank you for reading all this book!

If and when you decide to exercise your right, you should almost always do it at the expiration date and not before, because you'll lose the time value if you exercise early. When you alert your broker to this decision, it's also important to know that you cannot then change your mind–the decision is permanent.

You have already taken a step towards your improvement.

Best wishes!